"Reserve Duty: A Journey in Community Policing.

Foreword

The Garda Reserve is an intriguing facet of Irish law enforcement. A dedicated group of volunteers, they bridge the gap between the community and the Gardaí, offering invaluable support and a fresh perspective.

In this insightful small book, Seán, a former Garda Reserve member, offers a unique glimpse into the Reserve experience. His honest and engaging narrative sheds light on the motivations that drive people to join, the challenges they face, and the rewards they reap.

Whether you're considering joining the Reserve yourself, or simply curious about this dedicated group, this book is a must-read. Seán provides a balanced view, the sense of purpose, and the practical realities of being a Reserve member.

This book is not just a personal story; it's a valuable resource. It explores the training process, the day-to-day duties, and the dynamics within a Garda station. Seán also looks into the transferable skills gained through this experience, making a compelling case for the value of the Reserve program.

So, turn the page and embark on this journey into the world of the Garda Reserve. You'll gain a deeper understanding of this vital service, and perhaps even discover a hidden desire to contribute to your community in a meaningful way.

History

From Enforcing British Rule to Guardians of the Peace: A History of An Garda Síochána

The Garda Síochána, Ireland's national police force, boasts a history intertwined with the fight for independence and a shift towards community-based policing.

Predecessors and a Fresh Start:

Prior to the Garda Síochána, Ireland relied on the Royal Irish Constabulary (RIC), a force often seen as an arm of British rule. Following the Irish War of Independence and the formation of the Irish Free State, the RIC disbanded. Michael Collins, a key figure in the revolution, envisioned a new police force – the Civic Guard – established in 1922.

A Force of the People:

The Civic Guard, later renamed Garda Síochána (meaning "Guardians of the Peace" in Irish) in 1923, aimed to be different. Unlike the RIC, it was unarmed and recruited heavily from former members of the Irish Republican Army (IRA). This decision reflected a desire for a police force that served the community, not an occupying power.

Building Trust and Consolidation:

The early years were challenging. Tensions lingered from the Civil War, and some viewed Gardaí (singular: Garda) with suspicion. However, the Garda Síochána focused on gaining public trust. A key step was the merger with the Dublin Metropolitan Police in 1925, creating a unified national force.

Modernization and Challenges:

The Garda Síochána has constantly evolved. While remaining largely unarmed, it has adopted specialized units and increased training to tackle modern crime. The force has also faced its share of controversies, including accusations of heavy-handed tactics during the Troubles in Northern Ireland.

Looking Ahead:

Today, the Garda Síochána is a respected symbol of Irish law and order. It continues to adapt to the challenges of the 21st century, focusing on community policing and collaboration with the public. The legacy of the force lies in its transformation from an instrument of control to a guardian of the peace, a role envisioned by its founders nearly a century ago.

A Force From the Community: A Look at the Garda Reserve's History

The Garda Síochána, Ireland's national police service, boasts a unique support system: the Garda Reserve. This dedicated group of volunteers contributes to public safety as part-time members of the force. But how did this program come about? Let's look into the history of the Garda Reserve.

Legislative Birth (2005): The Garda Síochána Act of 2005 marked the official foundation of the Garda Reserve. This act envisioned a reserve force of roughly 1,000 individuals, constituting 10% of the regular Garda strength. The core purpose? To supplement the work of the regular Gardaí and provide an extra layer of security during times of need.

First Steps (2006): September 2006 witnessed the commencement of training for the inaugural Garda Reserve intake at the Garda College in Templemore. Just a few months later, in December 2006, these pioneering members graduated and became operational. Their initial deployments spanned stations in Dublin, Cork, Galway, and Sligo.

Challenges and Change: The Garda Reserve program hasn't been without its hurdles. There have been periods of decline in membership. However, the Garda Commissioner and the Minister for Justice retain the authority to define the Reserve's duties, ensuring their continued relevance in supporting the Garda Síochána.

A Community Partnership: The Garda Reserve embodies the spirit of community engagement. Drawn from the public, these volunteers bring valuable local knowledge and experience to the force. Their presence fosters a stronger connection between the Gardaí and the people they serve.

The story of the Garda Reserve is one of ongoing development. While the program has faced challenges, it plays a vital role in bolstering Ireland's police force. As the Garda Síochána evolves, the Garda Reserve will likely adapt alongside it, remaining a valuable asset to public safety.

Introduction

The financial crisis gripped Ireland, and public services felt the pinch. Garda recruitment was frozen, yet the need for community safety remained. It was during this time, with a strange sense of civic duty (perhaps the tidy towns could have been a better choice!), that I decided to join the Garda Reserve.

In my early 30s, I craved a new challenge. My day job lacked fulfilment, and I believed my youthful energy (well, somewhat youthful) would be an asset. The application process was straightforward: a meeting with the local superintendent, an interview, and a medical. Interviews were my forte, and with the government pushing for a 1,000-strong Reserve, selection seemed a formality.

The compensation – 204 hours a year for €1,000 – wasn't exactly enticing. But the challenge? That truly appealed to me. I've always enjoyed meeting people, and the Reserve promised an eclectic mix. There would be the early-twenties hopefuls, seeing the Reserve as a stepping stone to a full-fledged Garda career. There would be others like me, motivated by a desire to contribute to the community. And, inevitably, there would be a few whose presence left everyone scratching their heads.

Templemore, the Garda training centre, felt eerily quiet during the crisis. Trainers were scarce, and the physical training, while enjoyable, revealed my lack of stamina. One particularly memorable exercise involved striking a padded-up figure with an extendable baton good fun, and perhaps a touch therapeutic! Academics, however, were never my strong suit. Hours spent in a Sligo classroom culminated in a barely-passed test.

Finally, the call came, summoning me to the "bright lights" of Roscommon town (think Manhattan, but with a castle!). My first night shift – 10 pm to 6 am – offered little in the way of introductions. Just blend in, they seemed to say.

As in any workplace, the Garda Reserve had its share of characters. Some, primarily the female members, were a pleasure to work with professional, communicative, and blessed with common sense. Others, however, weren't so welcoming. Being left behind on calls due to a sergeant's absence spoke volumes of their perception of the Reserve: an unwelcome erosion of their roles. While I couldn't entirely disagree, my only desire was to contribute.

The good ones took the time to explain procedures and the rationale behind them. The not-so-good ones treated me like an unwanted child. In retrospect, I felt underutilized. Roscommon may not have been a bustling metropolis, but I knew I was capable of more. Committed as I was (I volunteered every second weekend and even covered New Year's Eve!), a seed of doubt began to sprout. One particularly slow 3 am shift brought a stark realization: "What am I doing here?"

Leaving the Reserve wasn't easy. Regret lingered for a few months, but I found a more fulfilling role in the volunteer sector. What did I gain from my Garda Reserve experience? A wealth of knowledge in a short period, a network of fantastic people, and a deeper understanding of the Garda as a workplace – with all its strengths and weaknesses. Looking back, I believe a twenty-year-old me, brimming with the right attitude, could have thrived in the Garda and climbed the ranks. But for someone in their thirties seeking a transformative experience, the Reserve offered limited opportunities to utilize existing skills.

Table of Contents

Foreword

Introduction

Chapter 1: Becoming a Garda Reserve

- 1.1 The Application Process
- 1.2 Training and Induction
- 1.3 Role and Responsibilities

Chapter 2: The Role of a Garda Reserve

- 2.1 Supporting Community Policing
- 2.2 Assisting with Public Events
- 2.3 Collaborating with Regular Gardaí

Chapter 3: Training and Development

- 3.1 Ongoing Training Requirements
- 3.2 Specialized Skills and Certifications
- 3.3 Professional Development Opportunities

Chapter 4: Community Engagement

- 4.1 Building Trust and Rapport
- 4.2 Connecting with Diverse Communities
- 4.3 Crime Prevention and Awareness

Chapter 5: Policing Challenges and Solutions

- 5.1 Dealing with Anti-Social Behaviour
- 5.2 Responding to Emergencies
- 5.3 Addressing Public Safety Concerns

Chapter 6: The Impact of Policing

- 6.1 Making a Difference in Communities
- 6.2 Supporting Vulnerable Populations
- 6.3 Promoting Positive Change

Chapter 7: Handling Difficult Situations

- 7.1 Conflict Resolution Skills
- 7.2 Crisis Intervention and Mental Health
- 7.3 Use of Force and Restraint

Chapter 8: Legal and Ethical Considerations

- 8.1 Legal Authority and Powers
- 8.2 Human Rights and Civil Liberties
- 8.3 Ethical Conduct and Professionalism

Chapter 9: Personal Experiences and Stories

- 9.1 Diverse Backgrounds and Motivations
- 9.2 Memorable Encounters and Moments
- 9.3 Impact on Personal and Professional Growth

Chapter 10: Impact on Personal and Professional Life

- 10.1 Balancing Commitments
- 10.2 Personal Growth and Development
- 10.3 Enhanced Skill Set

Chapter 11: Continuing the Journey

- 11.1 Embracing Lifelong Learning
- 11.2 Professional Development Pathways
- 11.3 Mentorship and Guidance

Chapter 12: Reflections and Future Directions

- 12.1 Looking Back: A Journey of Growth
- 12.2 Lessons Learned: Insights and Perspectives
- 12.3 Contributions Made: Making a Difference

Chapter 13: The Future of Policing

- 13.1 Evolving Challenges and Opportunities
- 13.2 Technological Advancements
- 13.3 Community-Centered Policing

Chapter 14: Pros & Cons

Chapter 15: Conclusion and Call to Action

- 15.1 Reflecting on the Journey
- 15.2 Embracing the Values of Service and Integrity
- 15.3 Recognizing the Power of Community Engagement

Career background

Seán O'Connor is a highly accomplished health professional with a diverse range of experiences and a strong commitment to making a positive impact in the field of health and well-being. Currently serving as a Project Manager in Arts & Health within the Health Service Executive (HSE), Seán is dedicated to exploring the intersections between creativity and health to enhance the well-being of individuals and staff.

In addition to his role in Arts & Health, Seán holds a significant position as a lay member on tribunal panels for the Mental Health Commission. This involvement allows him to contribute to the fair and just assessment of mental health cases, ensuring that the rights and well-being of individuals are protected.

Seán is also deeply passionate about road safety and has developed the Drive Aware Programme (DAP) as a means to effect positive changes in attitudes and behaviours related to impaired, dangerous, and careless driving. Through his program, Seán aims to promote responsible driving practices and reduce the risks associated with reckless behaviour on the roads. His dedication to enhancing road safety has led him to deliver the Drive Aware Programme throughout the country.

As the founder of Seán O'Connor Coaching, Seán offers personalized one-on-one coaching sessions and conducts training workshops and seminars. Leveraging his extensive knowledge and experience, he empowers individuals to overcome challenges, improve their well-being, and achieve personal and professional growth.

Throughout his career, Seán has held various impactful positions. He served as a Project Manager with the HSE National Clinical Programme for People with Disability, where he played a pivotal role in improving healthcare services and support for individuals with disabilities.

As a Task Force Manager in the HSE Drugs & Alcohol sector, Seán contributed to the development and implementation of strategies to address substance abuse issues within the community.

His previous roles also include serving as the Director of the Dyslexia Association of Ireland, where he championed the rights and needs of individuals with dyslexia, and as the Chairperson and Director of Pieta House, an organization dedicated to preventing suicide and providing support to those in crisis.

Furthermore,

Seán has a unique background in the legal field, having served as a sitting Magistrate/Justice of the Peace within Her Majesty's Court Service. He brings a profound understanding of the criminal justice system and leverages this knowledge to make fair and informed decisions.

Seán 's expertise extends to the field of addiction counselling, having worked as an Addiction Counsellor in both community and prison settings. He has provided vital support and guidance to individuals struggling with addiction, helping them on their journey towards recovery. Seán has also contributed to the provision of counselling services within the prison setting, recognizing the importance of addressing mental health needs in such environments.

Additionally, Seán has made valuable contributions to the criminal justice system as a Drug & Alcohol worker with Probation Services. His work in this capacity focused on assisting individuals in overcoming addiction, reintegrating into society, and reducing reoffending rates.

Media work within TV and radio has provided Seán with a platform to raise awareness about various health and social issues. He has utilized these mediums to educate and inform the public, advocating for positive change and promoting well-being.

Seán 's career began in engineering, where he embarked on a four-year apprenticeship as a fresh-faced sixteen-year-old. He gained invaluable experience working for a large multinational Oil and Gas company, further developing his skills and contributing to the industry.

With an impressive array of experiences spanning healthcare, project management, coaching, counselling, advocacy, and engineering, Seán O'Connor embodies a passionate and dedicated health professional committed to improving the lives of individuals and communities. His multifaceted background and expertise enable him to address complex challenges, inspire positive change, and empower others to reach their full potential.

And for further insights into Sean's career to date please visit LinkedIn

https://www.linkedin.com/in/sean-oconnor/

Here's a quick rundown of Seán's publications to date:

A Therapist's Guide to a Little Bit of Everything: Is a comprehensive and invaluable resource designed to support therapists in navigating a wide range of topics and issues they may encounter in their practice.

From Struggle to Strength: Resilience is a quality deeply ingrained in the human spirit. It is the remarkable ability to withstand adversity, recover from setbacks, and emerge stronger than before. In this book, we embark on a journey to understand the essence of resilience, its significance, and the profound impact it can have on our lives

Feck Off Anxiety: As someone deeply invested in the fields of Coaching and Counselling, I have witnessed firsthand the profound impact that anxiety can have on individuals, families, and communities.

Feck Off Overthinking: Looks into the intricate web of overthinking, seeking not only to comprehend its depths but to provide you, the reader.

Feck Off Depression: This book looks into the complex landscape of depression, unravelling its many facets and providing insights into its various forms, from major depressive disorder and persistent depressive disorder to the cyclical highs and lows of bipolar disorder.

Feck Off Stress: A guide that doesn't just help you cope with stress but empowers you to conquer it.

Leading in Healthcare Management and Leadership in the UK and Ireland: Exploring the intricacies of healthcare leadership and management, shedding light on effective practices in this ever-evolving field.

Leading with Purpose: A Guide to Being an Effective Chairperson in the Charity Sector of the UK and Ireland - Offering guidance to aspiring and current chairpersons, emphasizing the importance of purpose-driven leadership in the non-profit sector.

Empowering Voices: A Comprehensive Guide to Becoming a Freelance Contributor in Drug and Alcohol Addiction Journalism A resource for aspiring freelance journalists interested in covering the crucial topics of drug and alcohol addiction.

Breaking the Chains: A Comprehensive Guide to Addiction Counselling in Ireland and the UK - Shedding light on effective counselling techniques and strategies to support individuals in overcoming addiction.

Shattering Stigma: This book aims to provide a comprehensive section of mental health services in Ireland, looking into the intricacies of assessment, diagnosis, and treatment.

Embracing Dyslexia: Building Strengths, Overcoming Challenges is a comprehensive resource designed to provide readers with a thorough understanding of dyslexia from various perspectives, including educational, psychological, and personal.

Drive Aware: "Safer roads for a safer society" - This has been the driving principle behind the ambitious initiative known as the Drive Aware program in Ireland.

Empowering Change: A Project Manager's Perspective on the Disability Sector in Ireland: This comprehensive induction provides you with a strong foundation to navigate your role as a Project Manager in the disability sector.

Balancing Justice: A Magistrate's Journey - Sharing my personal experiences and insights as a magistrate, highlighting the challenges and rewards of serving in the legal system.

Mastering Life Coaching: A Comprehensive Guide for Professional Coaches - Equipping life coaches with the necessary tools and knowledge to empower their clients and facilitate positive change.

Clearing the Air: Smoking Cessation Services in the UK and their Benefits to Society - Advocating for the importance of smoking cessation and exploring the valuable services available to individuals looking to quit smoking.

Engineering Excellence: Unveiling the Potential of the Gas and Petroleum Industry' - An exploration of the gas and petroleum industry, revealing the incredible potential and advancements within this vital sector.

All of the above publications can be found at

https://www.amazon.co.uk/~/e/B0C8G4ZN94

Where you can contact him

Seán O'Connor Coaching

https://www.seanoconnorcoaching.com/

Drive Aware Ireland

https://www.driveaware.ie/

Chapter 1: Becoming a Garda Reserve

1.1 The Application Process

The first step to becoming a Garda Reserve is understanding the eligibility requirements. Here's a breakdown of who can apply:

Age: You must be a minimum of 18 years old and generally not exceed 60 years old. Exceptions for those over 60 may be considered on a case-by-case basis, particularly for individuals with valuable experience or specialized skills.

Citizenship: You must be a citizen of Ireland or a legal resident with permission to remain for at least three years.

Character: You must be of good character and pass Garda vetting. This involves a thorough background check to ensure your suitability for the role.

Fitness: You must be physically fit and meet the basic fitness requirements. The Garda Síochána does not disclose the specifics of the fitness test, but it's designed to assess your ability to perform the necessary duties without undue strain.

Education: You must have completed the Leaving Certificate (Irish high school diploma) or equivalent qualification.

Once you confirm eligibility, the application process is entirely online through the Public Appointments Service website https://publicjobs.ie/en/. There's no application fee, and the process typically involves:

Online Application Form: This form gathers your personal details, employment history, qualifications, and motivations for joining the Garda Reserve program.

References: You'll be asked to provide contact information for two referees who can vouch for your character and suitability for the role.

Garda Vetting: Following a successful application, your background will be thoroughly vetted to ensure you meet the Garda Siochana's high standards.

Example: Sarah, a 25-year-old marketing professional, decides to become a Garda Reserve. She checks the eligibility criteria online and confirms she meets all the requirements. Excited to contribute to her community, Sarah completes the online application form, highlighting her strong work ethic, volunteer experience, and passion for public service. She provides references from her previous employer and a community leader who can speak to her character. After submitting her application, Sarah undergoes Garda vetting, a necessary step before embarking on her Garda Reserve journey.

1.2 Training and Induction

Upon successful application and vetting, accepted candidates progress to the Garda Reserve training program. This comprehensive six-week course equips individuals with the knowledge and skills necessary to fulfil their role effectively. Here's a glimpse into the training curriculum:

Garda Law and Procedures: This section looks into Irish law, Garda protocols, and relevant legislation. Recruits learn about arrest procedures, search warrants, use of force, and human rights considerations.

Self-Defence Tactics: Garda Reserves receive training in self-defence techniques to protect themselves and others in potentially dangerous situations. This may involve physical manoeuvres, de-escalation strategies, and awareness of personal safety measures.

Human Rights and Ethics: The program emphasizes the importance of upholding human rights and ethical conduct in all interactions with the public. Recruits learn about cultural competency, fair treatment, and the importance of building trust within communities.

Communication Skills: Effective communication is crucial for Garda Reserves. The training covers active listening skills, conflict resolution techniques, and clear concise reporting methods, both written and verbal.

First Aid: Basic first-aid training is provided to equip Garda Reserves with the ability to administer first aid in emergency situations until medical professionals arrive.

Irish Language and Culture (depending on location): In areas with a significant Irish-speaking population, Garda Reserves may receive training in basic Irish language skills and cultural awareness to enhance communication and build rapport within the community.

Following the successful completion of the training program, a formal induction ceremony welcomes new Garda Reserves into the force. This ceremony provides an opportunity to meet fellow Garda Reserves, supervisors, and Garda officers, fostering a sense of camaraderie and belonging.

Example: Michael, a recently retired teacher, joins the Garda Reserve program. During the six-week training course, he finds the self-defence training particularly valuable, learning practical techniques to ensure his safety while on duty. Michael excels in the communication skills module, drawing on his teaching experience to hone his active listening and conflict resolution skills.

The training program not only equips Michael with the necessary skills but also fosters a sense of purpose and connection with his community. Following graduation, Michael attends the induction ceremony, feeling proud to be officially sworn in as a Garda Reserve.

1.3 Role and Responsibilities

Garda Reserves perform a variety of duties under the supervision of regular Gardaí. Here's a closer look at some of

Foot Patrols: Provide a visible presence that deters crime and fosters a sense of security within communities. Garda Reserves patrol designated areas, observing and reporting any suspicious activity, while engaging with the public and addressing any concerns.

Public Safety Assistance at Events: Garda Reserves play a vital role in ensuring public safety at various events, such as concerts, festivals, sporting events, and parades. This may involve crowd control, traffic management, access control, and assisting with any emergencies that may arise.

Community Outreach Initiatives: Building trust and positive relationships with the community is a key aspect of Garda Reserve work. Garda Reserves participate in community outreach programs, such as attending neighbourhood meetings, visiting schools, and engaging with youth groups. These interactions help break down barriers, encourage communication, and foster a sense of collaboration between the Gardaí and the public.

Collaborating with Regular Gardaí: Garda Reserves work hand-in-hand with regular Gardaí, providing support and assistance in various situations. This may involve assisting with investigations, traffic control during incidents, or providing backup during patrols. Effective teamwork between Garda Reserves and regular Gardaí ensures optimal public safety and efficient service delivery.

Example: Sarah, the marketing professional who became a Garda Reserve, is assigned to foot patrol her local neighbourhood. While patrolling, she observes a group of teenagers loitering near a closed shop. Using her communication skills learned in training, Sarah approaches the teenagers in a friendly and professional manner. She discovers they're simply waiting for a friend and reassures them about their safety in the area. Through this positive interaction, Sarah builds rapport with the teenagers and demonstrates the proactive role Garda Reserves play in community safety.

Chapter 2: The Role of a Garda Reserve

2.1 Supporting Community Policing

Community policing is a philosophy that emphasizes building relationships between the Gardaí and the communities they serve. Garda Reserves play a crucial role in supporting this approach in several ways:

Visibility and Accessibility: Their presence in neighbourhoods through foot patrols and community events increases the visibility of the Gardaí and fosters a sense of accessibility for residents.

Building Trust: Positive interactions with the public during patrols and outreach programs help build trust and rapport within communities. This encourages residents to report suspicious activity and cooperate with the Gardaí in crime prevention efforts.

Local Knowledge: Garda Reserves often live within the communities they serve. This local knowledge allows them to identify potential problems, understand community concerns, and tailor their approach to best address local needs.

Example: Michael, the retired teacher who joined the Garda Reserve, participates in a community outreach program at his local school. He speaks to a class about the role of Garda Reserves and the importance of crime prevention. During the interactive session, Michael encourages students to report any bullying or suspicious activity they witness, highlighting the collaborative approach to community safety.

2.2 Assisting with Public Events

Public events often require a significant security presence to ensure public safety and manage large crowds. Garda Reserves play a vital role in supporting these events by:

Crowd Control: They assist with crowd management, ensuring the safety and orderly flow of people, particularly in high-density areas. This may involve directing foot traffic, preventing overcrowding, and de-escalating any potential confrontations.

Traffic Management: Garda Reserves may assist with traffic control measures around the event venue, ensuring smooth traffic flow and minimizing congestion.

Access Control: They may be tasked with checking tickets, verifying identification, and ensuring only authorized personnel have access to restricted areas.

Emergency Response: Garda Reserves are trained to respond to emergencies that may arise during events, such as medical emergencies, lost children, or security breaches. They work alongside regular Gardaí to ensure a swift and coordinated response.

Example: A large music festival is taking place in the city. Sarah is deployed with a team of Garda Reserves to assist with crowd control. They strategically position themselves throughout the venue, monitoring the flow of people and ensuring everyone enjoys the event safely. When a minor argument breaks out between two attendees, Sarah utilizes her de-escalation skills learned in training to calm the situation and prevent it from escalating.

2.3 Collaborating with Regular Gardaí

Garda Reserves are not intended to replace regular Gardaí but rather to support and complement their work. Here are some ways Garda Reserves collaborate with regular Gardaí:

Routine Patrols: Garda Reserves may accompany regular Gardaí on routine patrols, providing additional manpower and acting as extra eyes and ears on the ground.

Investigations: While Garda Reserves cannot lead investigations, they can assist regular Gardaí by gathering information, interviewing witnesses

Chapter 3: Training and Development

3.1 Ongoing Training Requirements

To ensure Garda Reserves maintain their skills and knowledge, ongoing training is mandatory. Here's a breakdown of the typical training requirements:

Annual Refresher Training: All Garda Reserves must complete annual refresher training courses. These courses cover essential topics like legal updates, use-of-force procedures, first-aid recertification, and communication skills enhancement.

Specialized Training Opportunities: Garda Reserves have the opportunity to participate in specialized training programs based on their interests and the needs of their local Garda station. These programs could focus on areas like:

Scene of Crime Awareness: This training equips Garda Reserves with the knowledge and skills to identify, preserve, and protect potential evidence at crime scenes.

Public Order Management: This training focuses on strategies for managing crowds, de-escalating conflict situations, and maintaining public order during protests or demonstrations.

Interpersonal Skills and Conflict Resolution: This training further develops Garda Reserves' communication and conflict resolution skills, allowing them to effectively handle challenging interactions with the public.

Example: Michael, who enjoys working with youth, expresses interest in specialized training. He participates in a program on youth engagement and diversion strategies. This training equips him with the skills to connect with young people, identify potential problems, and encourage positive decision-making, contributing to crime prevention efforts.

3.2 Specialized Skills and Certifications

While not mandatory, Garda Reserves can pursue additional certifications to enhance their skillset and potentially take on specialized roles within the program. Here are some examples:

First Aid Instructor: Qualified Garda Reserves can train other Garda personnel and members of the public in first-aid procedures.

Search Techniques: This training equips Garda Reserves with the skills to conduct lawful searches for evidence or missing persons under the supervision of a regular Garda.

Advanced Communication Skills: This training helps Garda Reserves hone their communication skills in high-pressure situations, allowing them to effectively communicate with diverse populations and de-escalate conflict.

Example: Sarah, who excelled in communication skills training, aspires to become a Garda Reserve instructor. She pursues additional training and certification to become a qualified instructor for the Garda Reserve program. This allows her to share her knowledge and skills with new recruits, ensuring they are well-equipped for their roles.

3.3 Professional Development Opportunities

The Garda Reserve program offers opportunities for professional development that can benefit both volunteer work and personal career aspirations. Here are some examples:

Mentorship Programs: Experienced Garda Reserves can mentor new recruits, providing guidance and support as they navigate their roles. This mentorship fosters a sense of community within the program and allows knowledge to be efficiently transferred.

Conferences and Workshops: Gardaí and external organizations may host conferences and workshops relevant to policing and community engagement. These events provide Garda Reserves with opportunities to network with professionals, learn about new developments in the field, and enhance their knowledge base.

Example: Michael, leveraging his teaching experience, becomes a mentor to new Garda Reserve recruits. He shares his insights on communication, community engagement, and problem-solving, helping them adapt to their new roles with confidence. Additionally, Michael attends a conference on community policing strategies, gaining valuable insights into innovative approaches to public safety.

By engaging in ongoing training, pursuing specialized skills, and participating in professional development opportunities, Garda Reserves ensure they remain effective contributors to community safety and continue to grow both personally and professionally.

Chapter 4: Community Engagement

4.1 Building Trust and Rapport

Building trust and rapport with the community is a cornerstone of effective policing. Garda Reserves play a crucial role in fostering these positive relationships through various means:

Visibility and Accessibility: Their frequent presence in neighbourhoods through foot patrols and community events allows for regular interaction with residents. This accessibility breaks down barriers and encourages open communication.

Positive Interactions: By engaging with the public in a friendly, professional, and helpful manner, Garda Reserves build trust and demonstrate their commitment to community safety. Simple acts like offering assistance, answering questions, or providing information can leave a lasting positive impression.

Active Listening: Garda Reserves actively listen to residents' concerns and take their experiences seriously. This shows respect and fosters a sense of partnership in addressing community safety issues.

Cultural Competency: Understanding and respecting the diverse cultures within a community is essential for building trust. Garda Reserves who strive to learn about different cultural backgrounds can effectively connect with a wider range of residents.

Example: Sarah, while on patrol, observes a group of elderly residents chatting on a park bench. She takes the time to approach them, introduce herself, and inquire about any concerns they have about their neighbourhood. The residents share their anxieties about recent petty thefts in the area.

Sarah actively listens to their concerns, assures them that the Gardaí are aware of the issue, and encourages them to report any suspicious activity. This positive interaction fosters trust between Sarah and the residents, demonstrating the Garda Reserve program's commitment to community safety.

4.2 Connecting with Diverse Communities

Modern communities are comprised of diverse populations with varying backgrounds, needs, and experiences. Garda Reserves play a vital role in connecting with these diverse communities to ensure everyone feels safe and included:

Community Outreach Programs: Garda Reserves participate in programs specifically designed to connect with diverse populations. This could involve attending cultural events, visiting faith centres, or participating in youth programs in areas with high immigrant populations.

Language Skills: In areas with significant non-English speaking populations, Garda Reserves with language skills can serve as valuable bridges between the Gardaí and the community. Their ability to communicate effectively removes language barriers and fosters trust.

Respecting Cultural Differences: Garda Reserves demonstrate cultural sensitivity and respect for diverse customs and practices. Building relationships requires acknowledging and appreciating these differences.

Example: Michael, who has a basic understanding of Polish due to his neighbourhood's demographics, attends a community gathering organized by a local Polish association. He introduces himself to members in both English and Polish, demonstrating his willingness to connect with the community. During the event, Michael listens to concerns about recent vandalism targeting Polish shops.

He assures them that the Gardaí are investigating the incidents and encourages them to report any further occurrences. By actively engaging with the Polish community, Michael demonstrates the Garda Reserve program's commitment to inclusivity and safety for all residents.

4.3 Crime Prevention and Awareness

Garda Reserves play a proactive role in crime prevention and raising public awareness through various initiatives:

Crime Prevention Programs: They may participate in programs that educate residents on personal safety measures, home security tips, and recognizing scams or suspicious activity. This empowers residents to take an active role in preventing crime within their communities.

Public Information Campaigns: Garda Reserves may assist with public information campaigns to raise awareness about specific crime trends or safety concerns. This could involve distributing flyers, sharing information on social media, or presenting at community meetings.

Patrolling High-Risk Areas: Their presence in high-risk areas can deter criminal activity and provide a sense of security to residents. By being visible and approachable, Garda Reserves encourage reporting of suspicious activity.

Example: Sarah notices a rise in bicycle thefts in her neighbourhood. She works with the local Garda station to develop a public information campaign. They create flyers outlining basic bicycle security tips and distribute them throughout the community. Additionally, Sarah participates in a community meeting, presenting information on the theft trend and encouraging residents to report any suspicious activity involving bicycles. These proactive measures empower residents and deter potential crime.

By building trust with diverse communities and actively engaging in crime prevention initiatives, Garda Reserves contribute significantly to promoting a safer and more secure environment for all.

Chapter 5: Policing Challenges and Solutions

5.1 Dealing with Anti-Social Behaviour

Anti-social behaviour (ASB) encompasses a range of low-level, public order offences that can disrupt the quality of life for residents and create a sense of unease. Here's how Garda Reserves contribute to addressing ASB:

Visibility and Patrols: Their frequent presence in communities through foot patrols deters ASB and provides a sense of security to residents. This visible deterrent discourages individuals from engaging in disruptive behaviour for fear of being observed and reported.

Identifying Underlying Issues: Garda Reserves, through regular interaction with residents and community groups, can sometimes identify underlying factors contributing to ASB. This could be issues like lack of youth facilities, substance abuse problems, or social isolation. By recognizing these factors, Gardaí can work with social services and community organizations to address the root causes and prevent future occurrences.

De-escalation and Mediation: Garda Reserves are trained in de-escalation techniques and conflict resolution. When encountering situations of ASB like public intoxication or arguments, they can intervene calmly, mediate the situation, and prevent it from escalating into violence.

Community Engagement: By building relationships with community leaders and youth groups, Garda Reserves can foster a sense of ownership over community safety. This collaborative approach encourages residents to report ASB and work together with the Gardaí to address these issues.

Example: Sarah, while on patrol, observes a group of teenagers loitering outside a shop, using loud language and littering. Instead of resorting to confrontation, Sarah approaches them in a friendly yet firm manner. She reminds them of the noise ordinance and the importance of keeping the area clean. Sensing their boredom, Sarah suggests alternative activities available at the local youth centre. This calm and respectful interaction effectively addresses the ASB while also connecting with the teenagers and promoting positive community relations.

5.2 Responding to Emergencies

While responding to major emergencies falls primarily to regular Gardaí, Garda Reserves are trained to play a supportive role in such situations. Here's how they contribute:

Scene Security: Garda Reserves can be deployed to secure the scene of an emergency, cordoning off the area and preventing unauthorized access. This ensures the safety of emergency responders and bystanders while preserving potential evidence.

Traffic Management: In situations involving accidents or road closures, Garda Reserves can assist with traffic management, ensuring the smooth flow of emergency vehicles and minimizing congestion.

Public Assistance: They can provide assistance to members of the public affected by the emergency. This could involve helping evacuate residents, directing them to a safe area, or simply offering reassurance and a calm presence during a stressful situation.

Information Gathering: Garda Reserves can assist in gathering information from witnesses or bystanders in the aftermath of an emergency. This information can be crucial for the Garda investigation and ensuring public safety.

Example: Michael is on patrol when he witnesses a car accident at an intersection. He immediately calls for backup from regular Gardaí and secures the scene. Michael directs bystanders to a safe distance and ensures the injured parties receive medical attention. Once regular Gardaí arrive, Michael assists them by taking witness statements and gathering information about the accident. By acting swiftly and calmly, Michael contributes to a coordinated emergency response and minimizes potential risks.

5.3 Addressing Public Safety Concerns

Public safety encompasses a broad range of issues that affect the well-being of a community. Here's how Garda Reserves play a role in addressing these concerns:

Foot Patrols and Crime Prevention: Their regular presence in neighbourhoods deters crime and allows them to identify potential hazards or suspicious activity. By reporting these observations to regular Gardaí, they contribute to proactive crime prevention efforts.

Vulnerable Person Checks: In some instances, Garda Reserves may be involved in welfare checks on vulnerable individuals, such as the elderly living alone. This ensures their safety and allows for early intervention if there are any concerns about their well-being.

Community Safety Programs: Garda Reserves may participate in community safety programs, educating residents on topics like personal safety, fire prevention, or domestic violence awareness. This empowers residents to take an active role in ensuring their own safety and that of their community.

Example: During a foot patrol, Sarah observes a broken streetlight in a secluded alleyway. She recognizes this as a potential safety hazard, especially for residents walking home at night. She reports the issue to the local council and ensures a temporary solution is implemented until the light is repaired. By identifying and addressing this safety concern, Sarah contributes to a safer walking environment for the community.

By actively addressing anti-social behaviour, providing support during emergencies, and remaining vigilant to public safety concerns, Garda Reserves play a vital role in maintaining

Chapter 6: The Rewards and Challenges of Being a Garda Reserve

6.1 The Rewards of Service

Becoming a Garda Reserve offers a multitude of personal and professional rewards for those who choose to dedicate their time and energy to serving their community. Here are some of the key benefits:

Making a Difference: Garda Reserves directly contribute to the safety and well-being of their communities. Witnessing the positive impact of their work, from deterring crime to assisting residents in need, fosters a sense of purpose and accomplishment.

Developing Valuable Skills: The training and experience gained through the program equip Garda Reserves with valuable skills that can benefit them both personally and professionally. These skills include communication, conflict resolution, problem-solving, self-defence, and community engagement.

Building Relationships: Garda Reserves interact with a diverse range of people from their communities. This fosters a sense of connection and belonging, while also allowing them to build positive relationships with residents, community leaders, and fellow Gardaí.

Personal Growth: The challenges and responsibilities encountered while serving as a Garda Reserve encourage personal growth and development. These experiences can boost confidence, leadership skills, and the ability to remain calm under pressure.

Flexible Time Commitment: The Garda Reserve program offers a flexible time commitment, allowing individuals to volunteer their time based on their availability and schedules. This flexibility makes it ideal for those who want to contribute to their communities while maintaining other commitments.

Example: Sarah, a marketing professional who joined the Garda Reserve program, finds immense satisfaction in her role. She recently prevented a potential burglary by observing suspicious activity around a vacant house and alerting the Gardaí. Seeing the homeowner's relief after recovering their belongings reinforces Sarah's sense of purpose and the positive impact she can have on her community. Additionally, the communication and leadership skills honed during training have proven valuable in her professional career.

6.2 Challenges and Overcoming Obstacles

While rewarding, the Garda Reserve program also presents certain challenges. Here's a breakdown of some potential obstacles and how to overcome them:

Time Commitment: Even with flexible scheduling, dedicating time to volunteer patrols and training sessions requires commitment. Effective time management skills are crucial for balancing Garda Reserve duties with work, family, and personal life.

Emotional Stress: Garda Reserves may encounter situations that can be emotionally challenging, such as witnessing accidents, dealing with distressed individuals, or intervening in conflict situations. Learning healthy coping mechanisms and utilizing the support network within the Garda Reserve program is important for managing emotional well-being.

Physical Demands: Foot patrols and responding to certain situations can involve physical exertion. Maintaining a good level of fitness helps Garda Reserves perform their duties effectively and safely.

Shifting Priorities: Life circumstances may change, impacting a Garda Reserve's ability to volunteer their time consistently. Open communication with supervisors allows for adjustments to be made and ensures continued service within the program's capacity.

Example: Michael, a retired teacher, initially finds it challenging to manage his time between Garda Reserve duties and his involvement with his grandchildren. He discusses this with his supervisor and explores alternative patrol schedules that better fit his current commitments. This open communication allows Michael to continue serving the community while also prioritizing his family time.

By acknowledging the potential challenges and implementing effective coping strategies, Garda Reserves can ensure a fulfilling and sustainable volunteer experience.

Chapter 7: The Importance of Community Policing

7.1 Building Trust and Collaboration

Community policing is a philosophy that emphasizes building trust and collaboration between the Gardaí and the communities they serve. Garda Reserves play a vital role in this approach by:

Visibility and Accessibility: Their frequent presence in neighbourhoods fosters a sense of familiarity and accessibility. Residents feel comfortable approaching Garda Reserves with concerns or reporting suspicious activity.

Positive Interactions: By engaging with the public in a friendly, helpful, and professional manner, Garda Reserves build trust and demonstrate their commitment to community safety. These positive interactions break down barriers and encourage open communication.

Understanding Community Needs: Through regular interaction with residents and community groups, Garda Reserves gain valuable insights into local concerns and priorities. This knowledge allows the Gardaí to tailor their policing strategies to effectively address the specific needs of each community.

Problem-Solving Partnerships: Working collaboratively with community leaders, residents, and social services, Garda Reserves can identify and address the root causes of crime and social issues within the community. This collaborative approach fosters a sense of shared responsibility for public safety.

Example: Sarah notices a rise in graffiti vandalism in her neighbourhood. Instead of solely relying on enforcement measures, she adopts a community-oriented approach. Sarah works with local youth leaders to organize a community clean-up project and a mural-painting initiative. This collaborative effort not only removes the existing graffiti but also empowers young people to take ownership of their community and express themselves creatively through positive outlets. This initiative exemplifies the problem-solving partnerships fostered through community policing.

7.2 Proactive Crime Prevention

Community policing goes beyond reactive responses to crime. Here's how Garda Reserves contribute to proactive crime prevention:

Crime Prevention Programs: They participate in programs that educate residents on personal safety measures, home security tips, and recognizing scams or suspicious activity. Empowering residents with crime prevention knowledge reduces the risk of them becoming victims.

Identifying Potential Issues: Regular interaction with residents allows Garda Reserves to identify potential problems before they escalate into criminal activity. For instance, they may recognize signs of social isolation among elderly residents or identify areas with inadequate lighting that could attract crime. By reporting these observations to the Gardaí, proactive measures can be implemented to address these underlying issues.

Environmental Design: Garda Reserves can provide input on environmental design initiatives aimed at reducing crime opportunities. This could involve suggesting improved lighting in specific areas, advocating for better security measures in public spaces, or working with local authorities to address abandoned buildings that attract criminal activity.

Example: Michael, while on patrol, observes a group of teenagers loitering around a closed community centre after dark. He recognizes the lack of recreational activities for youth in the area as a potential contributing factor. Michael brings this concern to the attention of the local Garda station and suggests collaborating with community organizations to explore options for reopening the centre or establishing alternative youth programs. By addressing the root cause of the loitering, Michael contributes to proactive crime prevention efforts.

7.3 Building a Safer and More Inclusive Community

Community policing fosters a sense of shared responsibility for public safety. Here's how Garda Reserves contribute to this goal:

Promoting Social Cohesion: By connecting with diverse communities and fostering positive interactions, Garda Reserves help break down social barriers and promote a sense of unity within the community. This social cohesion strengthens the collective effort towards maintaining a safe and secure environment for all residents.

Conflict Resolution and Mediation: Garda Reserves are trained in de-escalation techniques and conflict resolution. They can intervene in minor disputes or arguments within the community, preventing them from escalating into violence. This promotes a peaceful and respectful environment where residents feel safe to resolve conflicts constructively.

Public Safety Education: Garda Reserves can participate in public safety education campaigns, raising awareness about crime prevention measures, fire safety, or personal security tips. This empowers residents to take an active role in ensuring their own safety and the safety of their neighbours.

Example: Sarah observes tension rising between a local shop owner and a group of teenagers who frequently gather outside his store. Instead of ignoring the situation, Sarah intervenes in a calm and respectful manner. She facilitates a dialogue between the shop owner and the teenagers, helping them understand each other's perspectives. Through mediation, Sarah helps resolve the conflict peacefully and fosters a more positive relationship between the shop owner and the young people in the community.

By building trust, collaboration, and a proactive approach to crime prevention, community policing, supported by Garda Reserves, contributes significantly to creating safer and more inclusive communities for all residents.

Chapter 8: Working with Vulnerable Persons

Garda Reserves play a crucial role in interacting with and supporting vulnerable persons within their communities. This chapter explores the importance of sensitivity, awareness, and appropriate responses when encountering individuals who may require additional assistance or protection.

8.1 Identifying Vulnerable Persons

The term "vulnerable person" encompasses a broad range of individuals who may require additional support due to various factors. Here are some examples:

Children and Young People: Children and teenagers, particularly those from disadvantaged backgrounds or facing neglect, may be more susceptible to exploitation or criminal activity. Garda Reserves need to be aware of the specific needs and potential risks faced by this population group.

Elderly People: Elderly individuals living alone or experiencing physical or cognitive decline may be vulnerable to scams, abuse, or social isolation. Garda Reserves should be alert to signs of elder abuse or neglect.

People with Disabilities: Individuals with physical, intellectual, or sensory disabilities may require additional assistance or face challenges interacting with the justice system. Garda Reserves should demonstrate sensitivity and provide appropriate support for people with disabilities.

Victims of Crime: People who have been victims of crime, particularly violent crime, may be experiencing trauma and require emotional support and guidance through the legal process. Garda Reserves can play a crucial role in connecting victims with available resources.

People with Mental Health Issues: Individuals experiencing mental health challenges may require specialized support and may be more vulnerable in certain situations. Garda Reserves should be aware of de-escalation techniques and resources available for those experiencing mental health crises.

8.2 Importance of Sensitivity and Respect

When interacting with vulnerable persons, Garda Reserves must prioritize sensitivity and respect. Here's what this entails:

Non-judgmental Approach: It is crucial to avoid judgmental attitudes and treat everyone with dignity and respect, regardless of their circumstances.

Active Listening: Taking the time to listen attentively to the concerns and experiences of vulnerable persons demonstrates empathy and allows for a better understanding of their needs.

Clear Communication: Communicating clearly and concisely, using language appropriate for the individual's understanding, ensures vital information is exchanged effectively.

Respecting Privacy: Maintaining the privacy of vulnerable persons and safeguarding any personal information disclosed is essential.

Example: While on patrol, Michael observes an elderly woman sitting alone on a park bench, appearing distressed. He approaches her in a friendly and respectful manner, offering assistance. Michael actively listens to her concerns as she explains she feels isolated and worried about falling victim to a scam. He avoids judgment and assures her that the Gardaí are there to help.

Michael provides her with resources for senior citizen support groups and information on how to identify and avoid scams. By demonstrating sensitivity and respect, Michael is able to connect with this vulnerable person and offer her much-needed support.

8.3 Responding to Specific Needs

The appropriate response to a vulnerable person depends on the specific situation. Here are some general guidelines:

Reporting Concerns: If there are immediate threats to the safety or well-being of a vulnerable person, Garda Reserves have a responsibility to report the concern to the appropriate authorities, such as social services or regular Gardaí.

Providing Information and Referral: Garda Reserves can provide information on available resources and support services tailored to the specific needs of the individual they encounter.

Offering Emotional Support: Sometimes, simply offering a listening ear and a reassuring presence can provide emotional support to a vulnerable person in distress. However, Garda Reserves should not attempt to provide professional counselling.

Example: Sarah encounters a young teenager loitering on the street late at night, appearing anxious and withdrawn. Sarah approaches her in a calm and non-judgmental manner. Through conversation, Sarah learns that the teenager recently ran away from home due to family conflict. While Sarah cannot offer solutions to the family situation, she provides the teenager with information on a local homeless shelter that can offer temporary accommodation and support services. By offering a safe space to share her concerns and providing access to resources, Sarah demonstrates a supportive response to this vulnerable young person.

By developing their awareness of vulnerable persons, prioritizing sensitivity and respect, and responding appropriately to specific needs, Garda Reserves can ensure they provide vital support and contribute to the well-being of these individuals within their communities.

Chapter 9: Personal Experiences and Stories

The Garda Reserve program is enriched by the diverse backgrounds and motivations of the individuals who volunteer their time. This chapter looks into the personal experiences and stories of Garda Reserves, showcasing the impact the program has on their lives and the lives of those they serve.

9.1 Diverse Backgrounds and Motivations

Garda Reserves come from all walks of life, bringing a wealth of experience and perspectives to their volunteer roles. Here are some examples:

Retired Professionals: Individuals who have retired from various professions, such as teaching, nursing, or business, often find purpose and a desire to give back to their communities by joining the Garda Reserves. They bring valuable skills and experience in communication, problem-solving, and leadership to the program.

Students: College students are another group increasingly drawn to the Garda Reserves. They are motivated by a desire to gain experience in law enforcement, develop valuable skills, and contribute to their communities while pursuing their education.

Community Leaders: Local business owners, religious leaders, and community activists often join the Garda Reserves to bridge the gap between the community and the Gardaí. Their existing relationships and understanding of local issues are valuable assets in promoting community safety and trust.

People Seeking a Challenge: Individuals looking for a challenge and an opportunity to step outside their comfort zones may find the Garda Reserve program fulfilling. The training, diverse situations encountered, and the chance to make a positive impact provide a rewarding experience.

Example: A local Garda Reserve unit reflects this diversity. Sarah, a retired teacher, utilizes her communication skills to de-escalate situations and connect with residents. Michael, a college student, brings a youthful perspective and enthusiasm to his volunteer work. Finally, Daniel, a local business owner, leverages his relationships within the community to foster trust and collaboration with the Gardaí. These individuals, with their distinct backgrounds and motivations, work together effectively to serve their community.

9.2 Memorable Encounters and Moments

Garda Reserves experience a wide range of situations throughout their volunteer service. These encounters can be challenging, heartwarming, or even humorous, leaving a lasting impression.

Preventing Crime: Witnessing a potential crime in progress and taking action to prevent it, such as apprehending a shoplifter or deterring a burglary, can be a deeply rewarding experience for a Garda Reserve.

Helping Those in Need: Garda Reserves may encounter individuals in crisis situations, such as someone experiencing a mental health episode or a lost child. Providing assistance and connecting them with appropriate resources can be a moment of significant impact.

Building Relationships: Over time, Garda Reserves develop relationships with residents within their patrol areas. These positive interactions, from helping an elderly person cross the street to simply having a friendly conversation, foster a sense of trust and connection within the community.

Example: During a routine patrol, Sarah observes a young boy crying on a park bench. She approaches him gently and learns that he has become separated from his parents. Sarah remains calm and reassuring while contacting the Garda station. Within minutes, the boy's parents arrive, overwhelmed with relief. Witnessing their reunion and the gratitude expressed by the parents is a memorable moment for Sarah, highlighting the positive impact Garda Reserves can have on the community.

9.3 Impact on Personal and Professional Growth

The Garda Reserve program offers not only the opportunity to serve the community but also fosters personal and professional growth for the volunteers themselves. Here are some ways Garda Reserves benefit:

Developing New Skills: The training and experience gained through the program equip Garda Reserves with valuable skills in communication, conflict resolution, problem-solving, and leadership. These skills can be beneficial in both their personal lives and professional careers.

Increased Confidence: Successfully navigating challenging situations and taking initiative in their roles can boost a Garda Reserve's confidence and self-esteem.

Greater Sense of Community: Working alongside other Garda Reserves and interacting with residents fosters a sense of belonging and connection to the community.

Enhanced Employability: The skills and experience gained through the Garda Reserve program can be attractive to potential employers, particularly in fields like security or social services.

Example: Michael, who joined the Garda Reserves as a college student, initially felt unsure of his abilities. However, the training and experience he gained boosted his confidence and communication skills. Michael leverages these newfound skills in his part-time job at a customer service centre and feels more prepared for his future career path.

The stories and experiences of Garda Reserves showcase the program's multifaceted impact. It provides a platform for individuals from diverse backgrounds to contribute to their communities while fostering personal and professional growth for the volunteers themselves. By serving their communities with dedication and compassion, Garda Reserves play a vital role in building a safer and more inclusive

Chapter 10: Impact on Personal and Professional Life

Becoming a Garda Reserve is a rewarding decision that can positively impact both your personal and professional life. This chapter explores the ways in which the program can enrich your overall well-being and career development.

10.1 Balancing Commitments

The Garda Reserve program offers a flexible time commitment, allowing you to volunteer your service based on your availability. However, maintaining a healthy balance between Garda duties, work, family, and personal life is crucial. Here are some strategies for successful time management:

Clear Communication: Openly discuss your Garda Reserve commitments with your employer and family. Setting clear expectations and scheduling patrols around your existing obligations helps ensure minimal disruption.

Time Management Skills: Develop effective time management skills to efficiently manage your time between work, personal life, and Garda duties. Utilize calendars, to do lists, and prioritize tasks effectively.

Flexible Scheduling: Explore flexible scheduling options with the Garda Reserve unit supervisor. Discuss patrol times that best suit your work and family commitments. Remember, flexibility goes both ways; be prepared to adjust your schedule occasionally to accommodate the needs of the program.

Example: Sarah, a marketing professional and a dedicated Garda Reserve, creates a monthly schedule that allocates specific evenings and weekends for Garda patrols. She communicates this schedule clearly to her employer and ensures her family commitments are met.

When unexpected situations arise, Sarah openly discusses adjustments with her supervisor and fellow Garda Reserves, demonstrating the importance of clear communication and teamwork.

10.2 Personal Growth and Development

Serving as a Garda Reserve is a journey of personal growth and development. Here are some of the ways the program fosters your well-being:

Increased Confidence: Successfully navigating challenging situations and taking initiative in your role builds confidence and self-esteem. The program empowers you to step outside your comfort zone and develop your leadership potential.

Enhanced Communication Skills: Through regular interaction with the public, you hone your communication skills, learning to de-escalate situations, actively listen, and effectively convey information to diverse audiences.

Problem-Solving Skills: Garda work often involves encountering unexpected situations. The program equips you with critical thinking and problem-solving skills, allowing you to make sound decisions under pressure.

Sense of Purpose and Community: Contributing to the safety and well-being of your community fosters a sense of purpose and belonging. Building relationships with residents and fellow Garda Reserves strengthens your social connections and fosters a sense of community spirit.

Example: Michael, initially a shy college student, joined the Garda Reserves seeking a challenge. The program helped him develop his communication and problem-solving skills. Michael now confidently interacts with residents, de-escalates conflicts, and takes initiative in patrol situations.

He feels a strong sense of purpose in serving his community and has built positive relationships with his fellow Garda Reserves.

10.3 Enhanced Skill Set

The training and experience you gain as a Garda Reserve equip you with a valuable skill set that can benefit both your volunteer work and your professional career. Here are some transferable skills:

Communication and Interpersonal Skills: The ability to communicate clearly, listen actively, and build rapport with diverse populations is essential for success in various professions.

Conflict Resolution and De-escalation Techniques: The skills acquired through Garda Reserve training in conflict resolution and de-escalation can be applied in numerous professional settings, such as customer service or management roles.

Leadership and Teamwork: Garda Reserves learn to lead by example, collaborate effectively with others, and function as part of a team. These leadership and teamwork skills are highly sought after by employers across various industries.

Problem-Solving and Critical Thinking: The ability to analyse situations, identify potential solutions, and make sound decisions under pressure is a valuable asset in many professional fields.

Example: Sarah's experience as a Garda Reserve, where she honed her communication and conflict resolution skills, proves valuable in her marketing role. She now confidently delivers presentations, negotiates contracts, and manages client relationships effectively. The leadership skills she developed through the program also empower her to take initiative and contribute creatively within her team at work.

By effectively managing your commitments, the Garda Reserve program offers a unique opportunity for personal growth and professional development. The skills and experiences gained can enrich your life in numerous ways, fostering a sense of purpose, enhancing your skillset, and contributing to a fulfilling career path.

Chapter 11: Continuing the Journey

The Garda Reserve program is not just a volunteer role; it's a springboard for continuous learning, professional development, and personal growth. This chapter explores the various avenues available for Garda Reserves to keep their skills sharp, explore advancement opportunities, and contribute even more effectively to their communities.

11.1 Embracing Lifelong Learning

The world of policing is constantly evolving, and Garda Reserves who embrace lifelong learning can ensure they remain effective contributors. Here's how to stay up-to-date:

Regular Training Updates: The Garda Reserve program offers ongoing training opportunities to refresh knowledge on legal updates, procedures, and best practices. Actively participate in these training sessions to stay current with developments in the field.

Industry Publications and Resources: Subscribe to Garda publications, law enforcement journals, or online resources to stay informed about emerging trends, crime prevention strategies, and best practices in community policing.

Conferences and Workshops: Attend relevant conferences and workshops hosted by the Gardaí or external organizations. These events provide opportunities to learn from experts, network with professionals, and gain new insights into policing practices.

Example: Michael, a Garda Reserve with a keen interest in drug awareness programs, attends a workshop on identifying and addressing drug-related issues within communities. He actively participates in the discussions and learns about new educational resources available for public outreach.

This workshop equips Michael with the knowledge to contribute more effectively to Garda initiatives aimed at preventing drug abuse in his community.

11.2 Professional Development Pathways

The Garda Reserve program can serve as a stepping stone for further career aspirations in law enforcement or related fields. Here are some potential pathways:

Garda Síochána: For Garda Reserves who desire a full-time career in law enforcement, opportunities exist to apply for positions within the Garda Síochána (Irish National Police Service). The experience and skills gained as a Garda Reserve can strengthen your application.

Security Services: The transferable skills developed through the program, such as communication, problem-solving, and leadership, are valuable assets in the private security sector. Garda Reserves can explore careers in security firms or corporate security departments.

Community Safety Roles: The Garda Reserve program fosters a deep understanding of community needs. This knowledge can be applied to careers in community safety, social work, or victim support services.

Example: Sarah's passion for community policing and her experience as a Garda Reserve motivated her to pursue a degree in social work. The skills she honed in communication, conflict resolution, and understanding social issues within the program proved valuable throughout her academic journey. Now a qualified social worker, Sarah works with vulnerable youth, helping them navigate challenges and make positive choices, demonstrating how the Garda Reserve program can serve as a foundation for a fulfilling career path focused on community well-being.

11.3 Mentorship and Guidance

The Garda Reserve program fosters a sense of camaraderie and provides opportunities for mentorship and guidance. Here's how to benefit from this support network:

Senior Garda Reserves: More experienced Garda Reserves can serve as mentors for new recruits, sharing their knowledge, experiences, and insights into navigating the program effectively.

Garda Liaison Officers: Garda Síochána liaison officers work closely with Garda Reserves, providing guidance, support, and ensuring effective collaboration between regular Gardaí and the volunteer force.

Peer Support: Building relationships with fellow Garda Reserves creates a support network where you can share experiences, challenges, and best practices, fostering a sense of camaraderie and mutual encouragement.

Example: Michael, a new Garda Reserve, feels overwhelmed by the amount of information during training. He seeks guidance from Sarah, a more experienced Reserve known for her patience and communication skills. Sarah becomes Michael's mentor, providing him with study tips, sharing resources, and offering encouragement throughout the training process. This mentorship empowers Michael to navigate the program with confidence.

By embracing lifelong learning, exploring professional development pathways, and seeking mentorship, Garda Reserves can ensure they continue to grow in their roles, maximize their impact on their communities, and embark on fulfilling career journeys within the Garda Síochána or related fields.

Chapter 12: Reflections and Future Directions

As you embark on, or continue, your journey as a Garda Reserve, taking a moment to reflect on your experiences and consider the program's future is valuable. This chapter encourages introspection on the personal and community impact of your service while exploring potential areas for growth and development within the Garda Reserve program.

12.1 Looking Back: A Journey of Growth

Reflecting on your experiences as a Garda Reserve allows you to appreciate the personal and professional growth you've achieved. Consider these questions:

Skills Developed: What skills have you honed through training and on-the-job experience? How have these skills benefited you in your personal and professional life?

Challenges Overcome: What challenges have you encountered as a Garda Reserve? How did you overcome these obstacles, and what did you learn from the experience?

Positive Impact: Can you recall specific instances where your actions made a positive impact on your community or the lives of individuals you encountered?

Example: Sarah reflects on her time as a Garda Reserve. She recognizes the significant improvement in her communication and conflict resolution skills, which have benefited her career and personal relationships. She recalls a situation where she de-escalated a tense argument between neighbours, preventing it from escalating into violence. This experience reinforces Sarah's sense of purpose and the positive impact Garda Reserves can have on their communities.

12.2 Lessons Learned: Insights and Perspectives

Throughout your service, you've gained valuable insights into community dynamics, policing practices, and the importance of collaboration. Consider these questions:

Community Needs: What are some of the most pressing needs or challenges facing your community that you've observed as a Garda Reserve?

Policing Strategies: What aspects of the Garda Reserve program have you found to be most effective in addressing community safety concerns? Are there areas for improvement?

Collaboration and Partnerships: How can Garda Reserves work more effectively with residents, community organizations, and other social services to enhance public safety?

Example: Michael reflects on his observations during patrols. He notices a rise in petty theft targeting elderly residents in his neighbourhood. He also recognizes the value of community engagement initiatives, such as neighbourhood watch programs, in deterring crime. Michael proposes organizing informational sessions for senior citizens on how to protect themselves from scams and theft, fostering collaboration between Garda Reserves and community organizations.

12.3 Contributions Made: Making a Difference

Garda Reserves play a vital role in building safer communities. Consider these questions:

Sense of Purpose: How has serving as a Garda Reserve contributed to your sense of purpose and belonging within your community?

Community Impact: In your opinion, how do Garda Reserves contribute most significantly to the safety and well-being of your community?

Future Aspirations: Do you have any aspirations for the future of the Garda Reserve program? How can it be further strengthened to serve the community even more effectively?

Example: Sarah feels a deep sense of purpose knowing she is making a positive difference in her community. She believes the visibility and accessibility of Garda Reserves fosters a sense of security and encourages residents to report suspicious activity. Looking towards the future, Sarah aspires to see the program expand its public outreach initiatives, particularly focusing on youth engagement programs to promote positive interactions with law enforcement and build trust from a young age.

By reflecting on your experiences and considering the program's future directions, you can become a more effective Garda Reserve and contribute to the ongoing development of a program that serves the community with dedication and fosters a safer Ireland for all.

Chapter 13: The Future of Policing

The landscape of policing is constantly evolving, driven by emerging challenges, technological advancements, and a growing emphasis on community-centred approaches. This chapter explores how the Garda Reserve program can adapt and thrive within this dynamic environment.

13.1 Evolving Challenges and Opportunities

The future of policing will likely be shaped by new and evolving challenges. Here's how Garda Reserves can be prepared:

Cybercrime: As our world becomes increasingly digital, cybercrime is on the rise. Garda Reserves can benefit from training in cybercrime awareness and prevention strategies to educate residents and collaborate with the Gardaí in addressing these issues.

Emerging Threats: New social and environmental challenges may emerge, requiring innovative policing strategies. Garda Reserves can maintain a flexible and adaptable approach, readily embracing new training opportunities to address these evolving threats.

Community Engagement: Building trust and collaboration with increasingly diverse communities will remain crucial. Garda Reserves, with their strong community ties, can play a key role in fostering open communication and understanding.

Example: Recognizing the rise of online scams targeting vulnerable residents, the Garda Reserve program introduces training modules on cybercrime awareness. Sarah, equipped with this knowledge, delivers informational presentations at senior citizen centres, educating them on how to identify and avoid online scams.

This proactive approach demonstrates the adaptability of Garda Reserves in addressing emerging challenges.

13.2 Technological Advancements

Technology can be a powerful tool for enhancing policing effectiveness. Here's how Garda Reserves can embrace these advancements:

Data Analysis and Crime Mapping: Utilizing data analytics and crime mapping tools can help identify crime trends and predict potential hotspots. Garda Reserves can be trained to interpret this data and adjust patrol strategies accordingly.

Communication Technologies: New communication technologies can improve response times, information sharing, and collaboration between Garda Reserves and regular Gardaí. Staying up-to-date on these advancements ensures efficient communication and a coordinated response to incidents.

Body-Worn Cameras: The use of body-worn cameras can enhance transparency and accountability within policing. Garda Reserves can be familiar with the protocols surrounding body-worn cameras, ensuring proper usage and data management.

Example: The Garda Reserve program incorporates training on utilizing crime mapping software. During patrols, Michael observes a rise in petty theft incidents in a specific area. He utilizes the crime mapping tool to confirm this trend and relays this information to the Garda station. This data-driven approach allows for a more targeted deployment of resources to address the issue.

13.3 Community-Centered Policing

Community-centred policing remains a cornerstone of effective public safety strategies. Here's how Garda Reserves can continue to contribute:

Building Relationships: Regular interaction with residents fosters trust and understanding. Garda Reserves can continue to prioritize community engagement initiatives, building strong relationships and acting as a bridge between the Gardaí and the community.

Problem-Solving Partnerships: Working collaboratively with community leaders, social services, and residents empowers communities to identify and address the root causes of crime. Garda Reserves can facilitate these partnerships and champion problem-solving approaches.

Promoting Social Cohesion: By fostering a sense of shared responsibility for public safety and inclusivity, Garda Reserves can contribute to building stronger and more cohesive communities.

Example: Sarah observes a rise in vandalism targeting a local community centre. Instead of solely relying on enforcement measures, she facilitates a dialogue between community members and youth leaders. This collaborative effort results in a youth mentorship program aimed at providing positive activities and a sense of belonging for young people, potentially reducing vandalism incidents.

By acknowledging evolving challenges, embracing technological advancements, and remaining committed to community-centred policing, the Garda Reserve program can ensure its continued relevance and effectiveness in the future.

Garda Reserves will play a vital role in shaping the future of policing in Ireland, fostering safer communities and building trust between law enforcement and the public they serve.

Chapter 14: Pros and Cons of Being a Garda Reserve

Introduction

Before embarking on the journey of becoming a Garda Reserve officer, it's essential to weigh the advantages and disadvantages of this role. In this chapter, we'll explore the pros and cons of serving as a Garda Reserve, helping you make an informed decision about whether this path is right for you.

Pros of Being a Garda Reserve

1. **Contribution to Community:** Garda Reserve officers play a vital role in supporting community policing efforts, helping to maintain public safety and enhance the quality of life for residents in their local areas.

2. **Professional Development:** Serving as a Garda Reserve offers valuable opportunities for personal and professional growth, including training, skill development, and hands-on experience in law enforcement.

3. **Flexible Commitment:** Unlike full-time Gardaí, Reserve officers have the flexibility to balance their policing duties with other commitments, such as work, education, or family responsibilities.

4. **Networking and Connections:** Working alongside regular Gardaí and other law enforcement professionals provides opportunities to build valuable networks and connections within the policing community.

5. **Sense of Purpose:** Many Garda Reserve officers derive a deep sense of purpose and fulfilment from serving their communities and making a positive difference in the lives of others.

Cons of Being a Garda Reserve

1. **Time Commitment:** While the flexibility of the role is a benefit, Garda Reserve officers are still required to commit a significant amount of time to training, patrols, and other policing duties, which can be challenging to balance with other responsibilities.

2. **Limited Authority:** Compared to regular Gardaí, Reserve officers have more limited powers and authority, which can impact their ability to respond to certain situations or carry out specific tasks independently.

3. **Risk and Exposure:** Policing inherently involves exposure to risks and dangers, including potential encounters with violent or dangerous individuals, which can pose physical, emotional, and psychological challenges for officers.

4. **Unpredictability:** Policing is inherently unpredictable, and Garda Reserve officers must be prepared to respond to a wide range of situations and incidents, often with limited information or resources available.

5. **Emotional Toll:** Dealing with the realities of crime, trauma, and human suffering can take a significant emotional toll on Garda Reserve officers, requiring resilience, coping skills, and support systems to maintain well-being.

Conclusion

While serving as a Garda Reserve offers numerous rewards and opportunities for personal and professional growth, it also comes with its share of challenges and sacrifices.

Ultimately, the decision to become a Garda Reserve officer should be based on careful consideration of the pros and cons, as well as an honest assessment of one's motivations, abilities, and readiness for the responsibilities of policing.

Chapter 15: Conclusion and Call to Action

15.1 Reflecting on the Journey

This book has explored the rewarding world of the Garda Reserve program. We've looked into the training, the responsibilities, the challenges, and the immense satisfaction of serving your community. As you consider your role as a Garda Reserve, take a moment to reflect on your journey thus far.

What initially motivated you to join the program?

What skills and experiences have you gained through your service?

How has being a Garda Reserve impacted your personal and professional life?

What are some of the most memorable moments you've had as a Garda Reserve?

Reflecting on these questions allows you to appreciate the value of your contribution and the positive impact you've made on your community.

15.2 Embracing the Values of Service and Integrity

The core values of An Garda Síochána service, fairness, and integrity are fundamental to the Garda Reserve program. As a Garda Reserve, you embody these values in your interactions with the public and your fellow officers.

Service: Your dedication to protecting your community and upholding the law exemplifies the spirit of service.

Fairness: Treat everyone you encounter with respect and impartiality, ensuring fair and just treatment for all.

Integrity: Maintaining the highest ethical standards and acting with honesty and integrity are essential for building public trust.

By upholding these values, you contribute to the positive reputation of the Gardaí and inspire trust within the communities you serve.

15.3 Recognizing the Power of Community Engagement

The Garda Reserve program thrives on the strong connection it fosters between law enforcement and the community. This collaborative approach is essential for effective crime prevention and building a safer Ireland.

Building Relationships: Regular interaction with residents humanizes the Gardaí and breaks down barriers. Strive to build positive relationships and create a sense of familiarity within your community.

Problem-Solving Partnerships: Working together with residents, community leaders, and social services allows for a more holistic approach to addressing public safety concerns.

Promoting Social Cohesion: By fostering a sense of shared responsibility and inclusivity, Garda Reserves can contribute to building stronger and more resilient communities.

Your commitment to community engagement is a powerful tool for positive change.

Call to Action

If you are considering joining the Garda Reserve program, we encourage you to take the first step. The Garda Síochána website provides comprehensive information on eligibility requirements, the application process, and the training involved. By becoming a Garda Reserve, you can contribute to a safer Ireland, make a positive difference in your community, and embark on a rewarding journey of personal and professional growth.

Remember, every Garda Reserve plays a vital role. Whether you are a seasoned volunteer or a prospective recruit, your dedication and commitment are instrumental in shaping the future of policing in Ireland. We thank you for your service.

Further Reading

"Guardians of the Peace: The History of the Irish Garda Síochána" by John T. Redmond

Provides a detailed history of the Garda Síochána, offering insights into its formation, development, and evolution over time.

"The Guards: A History of the Irish Police Service" by Kevin Street

Explores the history and role of the Irish police service, including the challenges and triumphs faced by members of An Garda Síochána.

"Policing in Ireland: From the Local Force to An Garda Síochána" by Conor Brady

Offers a comprehensive overview of policing in Ireland, tracing its origins from the local force system to the establishment of An Garda Síochána.

"The Thin Blue Line: The History of An Garda Síochána" by Jack McDowell

Provides a detailed account of the history and operations of An Garda Síochána, highlighting key events, milestones, and challenges faced by the organization.

"Inside the Guards: A Detailed History of An Garda Síochána" by Diarmaid Ferriter

Offers a behind-the-scenes look at the inner workings of An Garda Síochána, exploring its structure, culture, and role within Irish society.

"Guardians of the Peace: The Story of the Irish Garda Síochána" by Joe Joyce

Chronicles the history and achievements of An Garda Síochána, shedding light on the experiences and contributions of its members.

"Policing Ireland: An Oral History of An Garda Síochána" by Brian Hanley and Scott Millar

Presents an oral history of An Garda Síochána, featuring interviews with current and former members of the organization, offering firsthand insights into their experiences and perspectives.

"The Blue Wall of Silence: The Culture of Secrecy in An Garda Síochána" by John Mooney

Explores the culture of secrecy within An Garda Síochána, examining its impact on accountability, transparency, and public trust in the organization.

"Guardians of the Peace: The Role of An Garda Síochána in Irish Society" edited by Eugene McEldowney

Features a collection of essays and articles exploring various aspects of An Garda Síochána's role in Irish society, including its relationship with communities, its response to crime and public order challenges, and its role in maintaining public safety.

"Policing in Ireland: Challenges and Opportunities" edited by Mary Margaret Moore

Offers a multidisciplinary perspective on policing in Ireland, addressing key challenges and opportunities facing An Garda Síochána in the 21st century, and exploring potential strategies for enhancing its effectiveness and legitimacy.

These books provide valuable insights into the history, culture, and operations of An Garda Síochána, offering readers a deeper understanding of the organization and its role within Irish society.

www.ingramcontent.com/pod-product-compliance
Lightning Source LLC
Chambersburg PA
CBHW070409230526
45471CB00006B/2713